The Big Oceania
Companion Journal

Which biomes are in Oceania?

Fill the biome map with a different color for each biome.
You can use your Oceania Biome Cards or Puzzle as a reference.

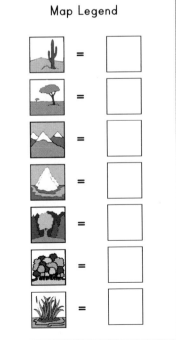

Map Legend

NAME _____

BIOME

It eats...

It lives in...

Its body is covered in...

It also...

NAME _____

BIOME

It eats...

It lives in...

Its body is covered in...

It also...

NAME _____

BIOME

It eats...

It lives in...

Its body is covered in...

It also...

It eats...

It lives in...

Its body is covered in...

It also...

NAME _____

BIOME

It eats...

It lives in...

Its body is covered in...

It also...

NAME _____

BIOME

It eats...

It lives in...

Its body is covered in...

It also...

NAME _____

BIOME

It eats...

It lives in...

Its body is covered in...

It also...

NAME _____

BIOME

It eats...

It lives in...

Its body is covered in...

It also...

NAME _____

BIOME

It grows in...

I wonder...

NAME _____

BIOME

NAME _____

BIOME

♪

NAME

BIOME

Made in the USA
San Bernardino, CA
17 September 2018